Appreciation for
Living Enlightenment

"Andrew Cohen's new book *Living Enlightenment* demonstrates a creative spiritual intelligence that breaks new ground in applying the spiritual wisdom of the East to the contemporary world. This innovative and energetic voice deserves your attention."   **RABBI MICHAEL LERNER**
Editor, *Tikkun* Magazine, author of *Spirit Matters*

"A series of penetrating, impressively concise, and often disarmingly personal questions about the spiritual life is here given answer by the remarkable Mr. Cohen. The wisdom he conveys is venerable, but his form is admirably fresh, vital, engaging. Anyone interested in inner freedom will learn much from this absorbing dialogue."
PHILIP NOVAK, Ph.D.
author of *The World's Wisdom*
Dept. of Philosophy and Religion, Dominican University

"*Living Enlightenment* speaks to me of dreams, revelations, mysteries and the still, small voice of the Intelligence ever awake in our unconscious depths. Who can resist this call?"   **ANN FARADAY, Ph.D.**
author of *Dream Power* and *The Dream Game*

"This book is a boon to the fearless, a gift to the sincere and a beacon to the lost. *Living Enlightenment* reads like a modern Upanishadic treatise. Andrew Cohen expounds his system of Gyana Yoga, the path of illumination through experiential knowledge, with great clarity and depth of understanding. May the knowledge conveyed in this teaching ever illumine the hearts of yogic aspirants, wherever they may dwell, in the East and in the West."
SWAMI NIRANJANANANDA SARASWATI
Chancellor, Bihar School of Yoga, India

"A superb presentation by the author of his own spiritual experience! An inspiration for others to follow faithfully the inner guidance that is theirs!"
THOMAS BERRY
author of *The Great Work*

"Andrew Cohen's new book, *Living Enlightenment*, is a very clear exposition and exploration of spiritual realization or enlightenment, the purpose of all spiritual pursuits. This book should inspire and encourage sincere aspirants on their journey toward this goal."

SRI SWAMI SATCHIDANANDA
Founder, Integral Yoga International and Satchidananda Ashram

"Andrew Cohen is someone with a passion for the Eternal Self—a passion for the infinite, as Kierkegaard would have put it, but really a passion for Enlightenment, for the ultimate consciousness that is awareness of the Eternal Identity unconditioned by the fleeting egoic identity. With a single-minded focus, his work is to open the door to that spaciousness of being that is who we really are."

WAYNE TEASDALE
author of *The Mystic Heart*

"Short, crisp, clear, and free of the jargon that one often hears and reads in Self-realization circles, *Living Enlightenment* is the reading equivalent of jumping into icy water—a sharp, bracing jolt to the whole system. It gives new meaning to the phrase 'wake-up call.'"

JACK CRITTENDEN, Ph.D.
author of *Beyond Individualism*
Dept. of Political Science, Arizona State University

"As always, Andrew's words pierce the nebulous and abstract and show us the clarity of his uncompromising demand to be who we actually are. Bravo!"

LEE LOZOWICK
Founder, Hohm Community
author of *The Alchemy of Transformation*

"If you are serious about finding a way out of the madness that the mind has distorted this manifestation into, you will find firm uncompromising help in Andrew Cohen's *Living Enlightenment*. To some very basic questions, it offers insightful precise answers, coming effortlessly from his personal intimate knowledge of the subject. His teaching is offered here in an Upanishadic question-and-answer format, allowing the reader to contemplate an answer to each question before reading Andrew's response. I urgently recommend an in-depth study of this offering.

RAMANAND PATEL
Senior BKS Iyengar Yoga Teacher

"Andrew Cohen is a true *tzaddik*, possessed, on the one hand, by a clear ontological vision and, on the other, by the gift of sharing it. Cohen's ontological reminder comes with an ethicist's concern for living right and helping the universe along, a perfect amalgam of Buddhist and Jewish practice. His writing is tonic and his teaching bracing. I was eight times kinder to myself and to everyone else after absorbing Cohen's tomette."

ANDREI CODRESCU
NPR commentator, author of *Messiah*

"To the committed and uncompromising spiritual aspirant, *Living Enlightenment* is a clear, fresh, and passionate call to wake up and take responsibility for the fulfillment of our highest human possibility."

MARIANA CAPLAN
author of *Halfway Up the Mountain*

Other books by Andrew Cohen

Embracing Heaven & Earth

Enlightenment Is a Secret

Freedom Has No History

An Unconditional Relationship to Life

Autobiography of an Awakening

In Defense of the Guru Principle

Who Am I? & How Shall I Live?

My Master Is My Self

foreword by ken wilber

living
enlightenment
a call for evolution beyond ego

andrew cohen

MOKSHA
P R E S S

Copyright ©2002 by Moksha Press
P.O. Box 2360, Lenox, Massachusetts 01240 USA
All rights reserved
No reproduction without permission from the publisher
Printed in the United States of America
Design by Moksha Press
Printed on recycled paper

Moksha Press Cataloging
Cohen, Andrew, 1955 Oct. 23-
Living enlightenment: a call for evolution beyond ego.
ISBN 1-883929-30-X
[by Andrew Cohen] Foreword by Ken Wilber.
1. Spiritual life. 2. Self-realization - Religious aspects.
3. Consciousness. 4. Absolute, The.
I. Wilber, Ken. II. Title.
291.4   BL624
Library of Congress Control Number: 2002100395

contents

foreword

When it comes to spiritual teachers, there are those who are safe, gentle, consoling, soothing, caring; and there are the outlaws, the living terrors, the Rude Boys and Nasty Girls of God realization, the men and women who are in your face, disturbing you, terrifying you, until you radically awaken to who and what you really are.

And may I suggest?: choose your teachers carefully.

If you want encouragement, soft smiles, ego stroking, gentle caresses of your self-contracting ways, pats on the back and sweet words of solace, find yourself a Nice Guy or Good Girl, and hold their hand on the sweet path of stress reduction and egoic comfort. But if you want Enlightenment, if you want to wake up, if you want to get fried in the fire of passionate Infinity, then, I promise you: find yourself a Rude Boy or a Nasty Girl, the ones who make you uncomfortable in their presence, who scare you witless, who will turn on you in a second and hold you up for ridicule, who will make you wish you were never born, who will offer you not sweet comfort but abject terror, not saccharin solace but scorching angst, for then, just then, you might very well be on the path to your own Original Face.

Most of us, I suspect, prefer our spiritual teachers to be of the Nice-Guy variety. Soft, comforting, non-threatening, a source of succor for a worn and weary soul, a safe harbor in the samsaric storm. There is nothing wrong with that, of course; spirituality comes in all sorts of flavors, and I have known some awfully Nice Guys. But if the flavor tends toward Enlightenment instead of consolation, if it drifts away from soothing dreams toward actually waking up, if it rumbles toward a God realization and not egoic fortification, then that demands a brutal, shocking death: a literal death of your separate self, a painful, frightening, horrifying dissolution— a miraculous extinction you will actually witness as you expand into the boundless, formless, radical Truth that will pervade your every cell and drench your being to the core and expand what you thought was your self until it embraces the distant galaxies. For only on the other side of death lies Spirit, only on the other side of egoic slaughter lies the Good and the True and the Beautiful. "You will come in due course to realize that your true glory lies where you cease to exist," as the illustrious Sri Ramana Maharshi constantly reminded us. Your true glory lies on the other side of your death, and who will show you that?

Not the Nice Guys and not the Good Girls. They don't want to hurt your feelings. They don't want to upset you. They are here to whisper sweet nothings in your ear and place consolation prizes in the outstretched hand of the self-contraction, balm for a war-torn weary ego, techniques to prop it up in its constant battle with the world of otherness. In a sense, it's very easy being a Nice-Guy teacher: no muss, no fuss, no wrestling with egoic resistance and exhausting confrontation. Be nice to the ego, pat it on the back, have it count its breaths, hum a few mantras.

Rude Boys know better. They are not here to console but to shatter, not to comfort but to demolish. They are uncompromising, brutal, laser-like. They are in your face until you recognize your Original Face—and they simply will not back off, they will not back down, they will not let up until you let go—radically, fully, completely, unhesitatingly. They live as Compassion—real compassion, not idiot compassion—and real compassion uses a sword more often than a sweet. They deeply offend the ego (and the greater the offense, the bigger the ego). They are alive as Truth, they are everywhere confronted with egos, and they choose the former uncompromisingly.

Fritz Perls, the founder of Gestalt Therapy, used to say that nobody comes to a therapist to get better (although they always say they do); they really come to perfect their neurosis. Just so, nobody comes to a spiritual teacher to get Enlightenment (although everybody claims they do); rather, they come to a spiritual teacher to learn more subtle and sophisticated egoic games—in this case, the game of "Look at me being really spiritual."

After all, what is it in you that brings you to a spiritual teacher in the first place? It's not the Spirit in you, since that is already enlightened and has no need to seek. No, it is the ego in you that brings you to a teacher: you want to see yourself in the presence of the spiritual game, you want to meet yourself tomorrow as a realized being—in plain language, you want your ego to continue into a spiritual paradise.

And what's a poor teacher to do, confronted with such egoic cunning? *Everybody* who comes to a spiritual teacher comes egoically motivated. And teachers have two choices in the face of this onslaught of the separate selves, this conference of the self-contractions: they can play to the audience, or they can blow the entire building up.

Andrew Cohen is a Rude Boy. He is not here to offer comfort; he is here to tear you into approximately a thousand pieces...so that Infinity can reassemble you, Freedom can replace imprisonment, Fullness can outshine fear. And that simply will not happen if all you want is consolation, soothing prayers, ruffle-free platitudes, "It will all be okay." Well, it will not be okay if you want Enlightenment. It will, in fact, be hell, and only Rude Boys are rude enough to tell you that, and to show you that—if you can stand the rudeness, stay in the fire, burn clean as Infinity and radiate as the stars.

Every deeply enlightened teacher I have known has been a Rude Boy or Nasty Girl. The original Rude Boys were, of course, the great Zen masters, who, when faced with yet another ego claiming to want Enlightenment, would get a huge stick and whack the aspirant right between the eyes. And that was just the beginning, that was the easy part; things got nastier fast—but at the other end of that brutality lay ever-present Realization, a shocking jolting death of the self and the radiant resurrection of infinite Spirit as your very own true nature: if you could stand the heat. Rude Boys are on your case in the worst way, they breathe fire, eat hot coals, will roast your ass in a screaming second and fry your ego before you knew what hit it: undo your self-contracting fear and sizzle your well-honed defenses: if you can stand the heat.

I have often heard Nice-Guy teachers say that Andrew Cohen is rude, and I think, "You don't know the half of it." I have often heard it said that Andrew is difficult, offending, edgy, and I think, "Thank God." In fact, virtually every criticism I have ever heard of Andrew is a variation on, "He's very rude, don't you think?" And I smile the biggest smile you can imagine. If it weren't for the Rude Boys and Nasty Girls of God Realization, Spirit would be a rare visitor in this strange land.

Andrew's magazine *What Is Enlightenment?*, for example, is the only magazine I know that is deeply, truly, outrageously Rude: which is to say, the only magazine asking the hard questions, slaughtering the sacred cows, and dealing with the Truth no matter what the consequences. The magazine is expressive of the very rudeness necessary to shatter egoic complacency, a complacency sick and thick, cloying, suffocating, drowning in its own self-smugness. You do well to be deeply offended by Andrew; he is, indeed, damn rude.

So, can you stand the heat? Or would you like more soft and consoling words of comfort, more consolation prizes for an Enlightenment that will continue to elude you? Would you like a pat on the back, or are you ready to be skinned and fried? May I suggest this? If you can stand the heat, you will indeed come to realize that your true glory lies where you cease to exist, where the self-contraction has uncoiled in the vast expanse of all space, where your separate self has been roasted and replaced by infinity resplendent—a radical

Release much too obvious to see, much too simple to believe, much too near to be attained—and your real Self will quietly but surely announce its Presence as it calmly embraces the entire universe and swallows galaxies whole.

In short, if you are ready to recognize your own Original Face, if you are capable of standing in the very middle of a raging fire that will melt your Heart and open it to eternity, then you have come to the right place. In the following pages you will see that Andrew Cohen is a Rude Boy who acts with uncompromising integrity, an integrity that shows compassion to your real Self and a very big stick to your ego. If you can stand the heat, then enter the real kitchen of your own soul, where you will find nothing other than the radiant God of the entire cosmos. For it is radiant Spirit that is looking out from your eyes right now, speaking with your tongue right now, reading the words on this very page, *right now*. Your real Self is glorious Spirit in this and every moment, and it takes a very, very Rude Boy to point that out and to stay in your face until you recognize your own Original Face, shining even here and now.

—*Ken Wilber*
Boulder, Colorado

preface

The implications of enlightenment are *always* revolutionary. The profound revelation of that which is Absolute, if it is deep enough to finally liberate, completely realigns our relationship to the human experience. But this simple truth tends to remain obscure for many seekers because the radical implications of enlightenment are so devastating for the separate self, for the ego. And many spiritual teachers these days seem to deny this truth, either because they haven't deeply realized it for themselves, or because they just don't want to threaten the status quo.

In the dialogues that follow, I have tried to convey the uncompromising yet ecstatically liberating perspective of enlightenment. And my purpose in this book is to clarify the truly revolutionary nature of that perspective in relationship to the human experience in the Western world at the beginning of the twenty-first century. My hope is that the timeless and always overwhelming impact of this revelation will be able to be intimately felt, intuitively known, and directly seen by the reader.

Once the call of the True Self is heard not only with the heart but also with the mind and conscience there will be no way back to the way things have been. Sooner or later we will recognize that we no longer have any choice but to allow ourselves the extraordinary freedom to go all the way in this life. Because after all, if we have begun to see through the illusory world that the ego creates and have heard the call of the True Self to live our lives for a greater purpose—what else is there to do?

– *Andrew Cohen*

what is enlightenment? 1

Q *Andrew, you are a teacher of enlightenment. A lot of people would like to understand what that word means. So, my first question for you is: What is enlightenment?*

A That's a very difficult question to answer in a simple, succinct way, because enlightenment means many different things on many different levels. Maybe I can begin by giving you one definition, and hopefully by the end of our dialogue together, a full picture of what it means will have revealed itself.

A good place to start would be this: One who is truly enlightened has directly experienced the ultimate or absolute nature of life itself. In that revelation, they have seen far beyond the boundaries of the personal self and discovered the universal nature of all their human experience. That explosive realization liberates the self from the perpetual tyranny of being trapped in a relationship to life that is merely personal.

Another way to answer your question would simply be to say that enlightenment is a condition in which the individual has come to the end of a fundamentally self-centered relationship to life. Most human beings, it seems, are concerned only with their own needs—constantly thinking about themselves, always wanting for themselves, perpetually lost in an endless, narcissistic preoccupation with their own personalities. So one way to understand what enlightenment is would be to say that it is a condition in which we have come to the end of this painfully self-centered relationship to the human experience.

How does this realization happen? Does it happen gradually, or is it a dramatic transformation that can occur in an instant?

It really depends upon the individual. But it doesn't matter whether it happens instantaneously or gradually. The only important thing is that *it happens*. Because as long as we are self-centered, lost in that which is merely personal, we are simply not going to be available. Available for what? Available to manifest the profound and extraordinary evolutionary potential that in most of us lies dormant. You see, this suffering world is in dire need of truly conscious beings—human beings who know who they are and why they are here.

But wouldn't moving beyond the personal in the way you are describing discount many important aspects of human life?

Absolutely not. The enlightened condition in no way denies any aspect of our humanity. It *enlightens* it. What does that mean? It means that our perspective dramatically deepens and widens. The perspective of one who has not awakened is limited by definition. The reference point for all of their personal experience is the separate ego. But the perspective of one who has awakened is free from this fundamental limitation because, as I've said, they have realized the absolute nature of life and the universal nature of their own human experience. And that changes *everything*. It transforms their relationship to being alive because the *context* in which they are living now infinitely transcends the merely personal dimension. Therefore, the question I encourage people to ask themselves is: *How enlightened is my perspective on my own personal experience?*

So an "enlightened perspective" would be one where we see all our experience in a much, much bigger context?

Yes. And that bigger context reveals itself automatically when we make the thrilling discovery that who and what we are, beyond the personal ego, is a profound mystery that is completely free from any sense of limitation. A truly enlightened human being spontaneously expresses that freedom from limitation *as their own humanity*. Indeed, simply through spending time in their company, we can awaken to that same mystery that is also our own true nature. In their reflection, it becomes obvious how, in our ignorance, we have been living in an alarmingly small context. And we see directly that it is that small context alone that creates the painful sense of suffocation and isolation that is so familiar in the unawakened state. The miraculous experiential discovery of the enlightened perspective is instantly liberating. And it is in this discovery that our humanity is finally set free to manifest its evolutionary potential without inhibition.

that which was never born 2

Q *You've used the word "absolute" a few times in your description of the enlightened state. What do you mean by that?*

A Absolute means free from limitation. When a human being directly experiences what enlightenment is, even if only momentarily, they find themselves infused with a consciousness that transcends time, a consciousness that was never born and therefore is free from death. I really mean that. They experience that which is immortal. And in that experience they discover a profound inner freedom because they are no longer fundamentally limited by the conditioned human personality that they have exclusively identified with since the body was born.

What do you mean when you say "a consciousness that was never born"?

If you and I were able to transcend any sense of being separate, individual, or unique, the state of consciousness we would find ourselves in would be identical. In the mutual recognition of that one consciousness, we would discover that we are the same One Self. In the consciousness of that One Self there is no time, no age, no memory, and no gender. Nothing ever happened there, and that is why there is perfect innocence and, in that innocence, a freedom from any sense of limitation. Again, that freedom is always untouched by anything that ever happened. So the reason that I said that this consciousness was never born is simple: The birth and death of any individual human being has no effect on it whatsoever. Do you understand?

Yes, I think so. As I listen to you, I get a sense of what you're describing—a sense of something beyond my personal identity. At times, when I sit by myself, I can experience the same state, but what always happens is that when I re-engage with my busy life, all of the confusing thoughts and feelings come back and I find that I'm still the same human being with all the same self-concerns.

But you see, you aren't questioning in a fundamental way what your relationship to your experience is based on. The state you're describing is very important. That sense of something beyond your personal identity is actually the Self Absolute beginning to emerge in your own experience as a tangible reality. But in spite of this, you still aren't questioning your prior conviction that you *are* the personality, the separate sense of self that was born in time.

So how would I do that?

The mystery that we're speaking about is always present when our attention falls away from the endless fears and desires of the ego. The more deeply we look into this for ourselves, the more we will become aware of this liberating truth. Underneath the ever-shifting sands of the human personality, that mysterious depth of our own Self that has no beginning and no end is always there. Most of the time we're simply not aware of it because our attention is perpetually distracted by the fears and desires of the ego. But our own Self never goes anywhere. And genuine spiritual experience *always* proves that to be the case.

So if, as you're saying, we are all actually the same One Self, what happens to our individual human personality when we have realized this?

If we are able to remain in the realization of that one timeless Self without wavering, then our personality will spontaneously become a vehicle for the manifestation of that One Self *in time*. The individual self will become infused with the presence of a powerful and transcendent singularity and will become a dynamic living expression of that which is absolute in this world.

But how can the personality be absolute? It's unique for every individual.

Of course the personality is unique. Relatively speaking, every individual is different, because he or she came into being at a particular time, in a particular place and culture. But that's not the point. I'm speaking about the potential for our unique personalities to express that which is absolute— that which transcends all differences.

But shouldn't we celebrate our differences—isn't that part of what being free is all about?

The freedom I'm speaking about, the freedom of enlightenment, is always only about the celebration of *no difference whatsoever*. That's why it's so powerful. You see, because most of us are so enslaved by the endless fears and desires of the separate ego, we are always striving to locate ourselves, always desperately trying to find out what it is about us that is unique. The separate ego's constant refrain is: "Isn't there something special about *me*?" But if we want to be free, if we seek for enlightenment in this life, then the relative distinctions that do exist between our personalities are not the things that should be most important to us. The only thing that should be important is winning our liberation from the ego's voracious need to see itself as being unique. Because after all, that need to be unique is the essence of what ego is. And our liberation from that need results only from the unequivocal discovery of the truth of who we are *beyond* the separate personality. As I said, when we make that discovery, our personality will become infused with the mysterious presence of the Self Absolute. And in contrast with the end-less negativity, small-mindedness, and self-centered desires of the separate ego, the Self Absolute is utterly wholesome. In that Self, there is freedom from the relentless narcissism of the ego and, because of that, there is ecstatic liberation from the unending existential tension that it constantly generates.

So, who will we be and how will we be as a separate personality when we have no need to see ourselves as being different or special in any way whatsoever? The answer is that *we will never know*. Who we will be then will always remain unknown to us. That's what is so extraordinary about this. The very part of us that wants to know will never be able to know the answer.   •

Did you say we will never *be able to know?*

The narcissistic ego always wants to know who we are when we look in the mirror. But when we die into our own True Self and recognize ourselves to be that which is impersonal and absolute, we stumble upon the miracle of enlightenment. We find that the Self that we have discovered is a mystery that cannot be seen with the eye and cannot be recognized by the mind. And that is why, if we want to truly know that Self, we have to be willing to *not see* it with our eyes and *not know* it with our mind. You see, if we want to be free, we actually have to let go of the very thing that we want to know in order to truly know it. We have to be willing to forget ourselves utterly and die into that ungraspable mystery. And from then on, we have to always be willing to live in a state of unknowing, a state in which we don't know who we are.

the perfect response 3

Q *Andrew, I have a simple question:* How *do we get there?* *Is the path to enlightenment just a matter of daily spiritual* *practice?*

A Well, if enlightened consciousness is what one is aspiring to, then "daily spiritual practice" alone will never be enough. If we want to be truly free, only total *surrender,* unconditional surrender, is the way, the path, and the goal. In the end there is literally nothing else to do but give up. Give up *completely.* Surrender your personal will to the always unknown, ever-inconceivable will of that which has created this universe and everything in it, and then just see what happens...

Just see what happens?

Yes. But never forget, true surrender takes guts, love, and incredible devotion. More guts, love, and devotion than most of us are ready to give just yet. But when we no longer have any choice, when we are compelled to submit to our own heart's deepest yearning for emancipation, then the real meaning of spiritual practice will become clear to us. Indeed, when surrender has become the foundation of our relationship to all of our experience, the very ground we walk on, then meditation and contemplation will spontaneously emerge as our closest friends and our most trusted allies.

How would you define meditation and contemplation?

Meditation is that state of consciousness that reveals itself when we take no position in relationship to thought. When we take no position in relationship to thought, the whole world and everything in it, including our own mind, falls away from us. Our experience is one of ecstatic freedom from boundaries, of finding ourselves blissfully alone, happily lost deep in the unknown. And if we can continue to resist the temptation to take any position in relationship to the arising of thought, we will find ourselves in a place that is impossible to describe in words. A place that is completely free. It is a place empty of mind and memory, a place of perfect fullness and perfect stillness. It is a place where nothing ever happened.

Contemplation is the deliberate and focused use of the mind in the service of the inspired passion of awakened consciousness. It is the movement of a mind that has been grounded in profound surrender. A mind that now naturally aspires to know the true and right relationship of all things, that ever strives to make sense out of the insecurity of the human experience in light of the ongoing revelation of perfect fullness. Ultimately, the movement of contemplation is a spontaneous effort, a consistently evolutionary response to life in the present moment.

Which practice is more important—meditation or contemplation?

I put great emphasis on the necessity of pursuing both meditation and contemplation simultaneously. But the way this works is very delicate. For a perfect result, we have to learn how to practice meditation and contemplation in such a way that one informs the other. Ideally, what that means is that the deeper our experience of meditation, of no relationship to thought, the more room there will be inside us for the unfolding of liberating insight when we begin to contemplate the nature of things.

But always remember, spiritual practice that is not grounded in a strong foundation of profound surrender will be virtually impotent in its capacity to enlighten us. Surrender and surrender alone is the key to the kingdom.

And how do I surrender?

Focus all of your attention upon the painful truth of your own psychological, emotional, and spiritual predicament. Face it with an unwavering intensity until the hard shell that protects your heart begins to break wide open. Then find the courage to let go of your mind completely—just let it go and let it go and let it go until there is nothing left.

And then?

If you're lucky, that will be the end of the story.

And when the story ends, does that mean that all my questions are answered?

Yes and no. Yes, on the most fundamental, existential level, your questions will be answered because when your heart breaks, you experience an inconceivable, mind-transcending love that reveals a breathtaking mystery that abides beyond time. That experience *is* the answer that sets all of us free from the fundamental belief that there's a question that needs to be answered, a problem that needs to be solved. But you see, at the same time—and this is the exciting part—the incredible freedom found in that mystery actually *enables* us to begin to inquire into the meaning of existence in a completely different way than we ever could have before. Why? Because now the starting point of our inquiry is one of deep conviction rather than debilitating doubt. And that changes absolutely everything.

So from that place of deep conviction, what's the most important question to inquire into?

Okay, it's a big one… It's the one ongoing question that my entire teaching revolves around: "What is the relationship between *nothing* and *something*?" What is the relationship between the unchanging, unmanifest, primordial Self and the ever-changing manifest world of time and space?

And do you know the answer?

Well, ideally, for a human being who is fully enlightened, the relationship between nothing and something would be *a perfect response.*

A perfect response?

Yes. A perfect response to life. You see, *that's what enlightenment is.* A perfect response. That's when there is no longer any distinction between the inherent perfection of the Self Absolute and that response that is its expression in the world of time and space. The question, "What is the relationship between nothing and something?" instantly points us to that same place of inherent perfection inside us all—and calls for a response. Even though most of us aren't aware of it, everything that we do and the way that we do it reveals how profound our knowledge of that place actually is and how deeply we abide there. So, in the end, "What is the relationship between nothing and something?" is the most important question because it not only points us to that perfection beyond duality but it also dares us to express that perfection as ourselves, so that the inner and the outer can truly become one.

one without a second   4

Q *For someone to be qualified to give all these answers about enlightenment, obviously they must believe that they're enlightened. So, Andrew—are you enlightened?*

A I never answer that kind of question.

Why not?

It's not the politically correct thing to do! You know, it's a funny thing—I have never been one to go around proclaiming that I am enlightened but, in spite of that, I have been accused of this terrible crime ever since I started teaching. You see, the reason it's better not to speak about these things is that people tend to misunderstand and get the wrong idea. Of course, if I didn't feel qualified to do what I am doing, I wouldn't dare to do it. But there's no reason that you should take my word for it. That is something you would be able to determine only by getting to know me. That's why I hesitate to make any bold declarations. I think that if we want to know what any teacher is really made of—if they're authentic or not—the only way to find out for ourselves is to get to know them.

For example, I'm sitting here with you, speaking with a reasonable degree of confidence about that which is absolute. And these kinds of questions naturally arise: Who *is* this person? What is the spiritual realization that they are describing? And what does that realization mean about their humanity? Because in the end, only the teacher's ability to actually *live* their teaching will convince us of their authenticity. After all, it has been this simple but ultimate challenge that so many who have claimed enlightenment have been unable to meet.

Why is it so challenging?

Because the implications of what we're speaking about here are so big. You see, initially enlightenment requires an individual to take a radical leap into the unknown. That leap is the timeless thrill of leaving the whole world and everyone in it behind forever. It's the death of the one who has a personal story; the end of their attachment to everything that their historical identity represents in time. It means saying good-bye to life as they have known it. It means that from now on they will be alone with their own Self.

So, that's the leap and it's an enormous one. But once that leap has been taken, the stability of the transformation depends entirely upon *remaining* resolutely in the unknown, never to return again. What does that mean? It means ever abiding in that mysterious place where the mind has no foothold whatsoever. It means always wanting to be nobody more than we want to be somebody. And most importantly, it means that we have surrendered our every breath to the Self Absolute and to the evolutionary impulse that emerges from that Self with a miraculous power to do what can't be done and to say what can't be said for a cause that cannot be imagined. There are very few who are willing to go that far. Indeed, even among those who appear to be seriously interested in these matters, when push comes to shove, most are not yet willing to surrender to the extent necessary for this kind of total transformation to occur. And the simple reason for that is that the degree of humility it demands is almost unimaginable.

Why is humility so important?

In this profound leap beyond the known, the individual recognizes that their true identity is not the separate personality but is, in fact, the Self Absolute or the *One without a second*. And of course, there could only be one One without a second. That is why humility is so, so important. Because unless the individual's motivation is pure, the temptation to claim the realization that "I am that One without a second" for the ego, for the part of themselves that may still want to be someone special, someone unique, will be irresistible.

The ego can claim enlightenment for itself?

Yes, and unfortunately it often does. But if the individual's motivation is pure, if there is a foundation of deep and profound humility, then the realization will not be corrupted by the desire for personal gain—and that's very rare indeed.

the status quo cannot contain it   5

Q   *You've been speaking about a "leap beyond the known,"*
which you said means the death of personal history. Wouldn't
this create some serious problems in our human relationships?
For example, you have a wife; I have a mother. What if I say that
I can't make this leap because I would still want to call my
mother on Mother's Day?

A   Do you think that when Jesus said to his disciples,
"Leave everything behind and follow me," their response
was, "But can we call our mothers on Mother's Day?"

You're asking a good question though. Even a lot of very
sophisticated people today don't seem to understand how big
enlightenment really is. They have somehow gotten the
strange idea into their heads that the explosive implications of
higher consciousness are something that they can fit neatly
and safely into the unconscious and ego-driven lives that
they are already living. The whole point is that *the realization*
of enlightenment completely destroys the status quo. It blows it
to pieces. If you are lucky enough to actually succeed in your
quest for liberation in this life then you will become a completely transformed human being and, believe me, you will be

seeing things very differently. You simply cannot squeeze the limitation-shattering perspective of enlightened consciousness into the way things have been in the past. It's far too big for that. The status quo will *never* be able to contain it. If the idea of calling your mother on Mother's Day is more important to you than your own liberation in this life, then you're obviously not seriously interested in the extraordinary possibility that I'm pointing to.

So are you saying that if I want to be enlightened I have to literally leave the world behind? In other words, just walk out of my house and leave my cat and my partner and shave my head and sit under a tree?

No, I'm not saying that. I'm saying that genuine spiritual awakening absolutely threatens the status quo of a world that is built upon the endless fears and desires of the ego. Enlightenment is the biggest threat that there could possibly be to that world. But in the modern spiritual marketplace, this all-important fact too often seems to be overlooked. Indeed, in the name of spiritual transformation, many of us are devoting a lot of our time and attention to improving ourselves, without questioning the ultimate validity of the self that's being improved, or even beginning to question the entire worldview within which that self exists. How many of us have cultivated the courage or awakened interest to seriously question many of the accepted cultural injunctions that, for most of us, end up defining the way we choose to live our lives? The point is, how truly liberated is our own mind? How vast is our perspective? Is our interest in enlightened consciousness so inspired that we always seek for a way of seeing that is free from unexamined assumptions?

You see, what I'm trying to say is that as much as we may believe we want to, we'll never be able to truly evolve in hell. Do you know what hell is? *Hell is not even knowing that we are lost.* Hell is being unconscious, adrift in the inner world of isolation and suffocation that is created by a self that is enslaved by the separate ego. And unless we become aware of how bad it really is, we'll never find the courage or the inspiration to do whatever is necessary to finally liberate ourselves here and now in this very life. I can't emphasize enough how urgent this is. So few of us take the possibility of our own liberation deadly seriously. And the main reason for this is, once again, that we just don't know how bad things are.

Andrew, to be honest, I don't think I'm at all in touch with the fact that I'm apparently so completely lost in the hell that you've just described.

That's because you have not yet reached that point in your own evolution where you want to be free more than anything else. You see, it is that *interest* in liberation alone that makes it possible for us to begin to see everything in a completely different light. And that interest, if pursued with passion, commitment, and the willingness to take enormous risks, has the power to catapult us into a radically different relationship to the human experience—one in which we will no longer be merely trying to fit in. Endeavoring wholeheartedly to come to terms with what it means to be truly alive, we will be actively pursuing the questions: *Who am I?* and *How shall I live?* as if our life depended on it. And my point is that the life-transforming, revolutionary perspective that is revealed through this kind of inspired questioning simply cannot be contained by the status quo.

So do you think it's not possible to get enlightened and still be a father or a mother—to live an ordinary life and yet seek for enlightenment at the same time?

Did you say in your spare time? Just kidding! No, being a father or a mother in no way needs to be an obstacle to the state of consciousness I'm speaking about. But as long as the *idea* of being a father or the *idea* of being a mother is more important to us than realizing this liberated state of consciousness, then the revolutionary perspective I'm describing will never be able to emerge in the field of our own awareness. As long as we are blindly attached to and unconsciously enslaved by *any* idea that is the expression of the fears and desires of the individual or collective ego, which is the mind of the world that we're living in, it will be impossible to live a truly liberated human life.

As I've been saying, so many of us are just trying to fit in, trying to survive the best we can. We don't know what else to do. At times, we desperately seek for a way to give our lives a sense of meaning and purpose. But *where* do we look? And *how deeply* do we question? Usually not too high, and not too deeply, for fear that the very foundation of our worldview, the very ground under our feet, may fall away if we even momentarily see through the illusion of security, stability, and permanence that the ego strives at all costs to constantly create. So we end up doing more or less exactly what everyone else is doing: believing, in our collective ignorance, that we are doing the best we can and that life is hard enough as it is without having to assume the burden of our own (and ultimately everyone else's) potential liberation.

I find the passionate questioning that you have been describing very inspiring, but when you speak about the ground under my feet falling away this makes me feel insecure to say the least. It just seems like too much.

The truth *is* too much—that's the whole point. The truth that liberates is too much for this mundane world of compromise and superficiality. That's just the way it is. That's the way it always has been, and the way it always will be. That's what is so powerful about direct spiritual experience. It literally has the power to destroy the world as we know it and reveal to us a completely different picture of reality.

And so what will our life look like then?

What will our life *look* like? Well, it will look FREE—free and unencumbered in a way that will shock and surprise most people. Our spirit, joy, and confidence in life will be irrepressible and uncontainable. Who we are, how we are, and the life that we live will embody and express the liberating truth that we have found in the spiritual experience. Our very cells will shout out and declare that truth to the sleeping world around us. Do you get a sense of what I'm pointing to?

Yes, I'm beginning to, and it scares me!

You shouldn't be scared; you should be inspired. What I'm describing is true fulfillment.

revelation and awakening   6

Q *Andrew, can you speak about your own realization—
how this occurred and what the journey was like?*

A When I was sixteen, I had an experience of cosmic
consciousness that occurred spontaneously. Completely un-
sought, it emerged from the unknown. I was sitting up late
one evening speaking with someone and suddenly, for no
apparent reason, the doors of perception opened. In an
instant, all boundaries disappeared and it literally seemed as
if there were no walls, as if I wasn't sitting in a room having
a conversation, but I was sitting in the middle of infinite
space. I could see the walls and I could see the room that I
was in but, inwardly, my experience was that all boundaries
were gone and I was actually existing *in and as* infinite space.
It became clear to me at that moment that there is only one
point in space and that, no matter where we may appear to be
physically located at any time, we will always be in exactly
the same place.

I saw in a way that is difficult to put into words that all of
life is One—that the whole universe and everything that
exists within it, seen and unseen, known and unknown, is

one conscious, glorious, intelligent Being that is self-aware. Its nature is Love but it is a love that is so overwhelming in its intensity that even to experience the faintest hint of it is almost unbearable for the human body. I saw in that moment that there is no such thing as death, that life has no beginning and no end. I was awestruck and overwhelmed. Tears were rolling down my cheeks and yet I wasn't crying and, strangely, my throat was opening and closing by itself. I was just sitting there but I felt like I was on my knees. I was in a state of wonder. And then something curious happened—I don't exactly know how to explain it. There was a message for me that said: "If you give your life to me and me alone, you'll have nothing to fear." And the implication was that if I didn't, then I would suffer terribly.

In what way did this experience change your life?

I had no particular religious convictions at that point because I had been brought up an atheist, but I was obviously deeply impacted by this unexpected revelation. In those few moments, I had been in touch with something that was utterly real. Infinitely more real than anything I had ever experienced before. As a matter of fact, it seemed as if I had been dead my whole life, in contrast with the event that had just occurred. For that very brief period I was awake; I was truly alive for the first time. This I knew without any doubt.

But after this happened I didn't know what to do about it. I began to read a little bit and I had some sense that I'd had a spiritual experience but I didn't know how to respond to what had been revealed to me. I was young and had intended to become a musician so that's what I pursued. But after several years, what had happened began to haunt me. The memory of that experience began to surface in my consciousness, and I felt that I was being called, that there was a demand to respond. Eventually, I made a decision that I was going to do just that.

I gave up the idea of becoming a musician and dedicated myself to finding my way back to what it was that had touched me so deeply. I began to practice different spiritual disciplines. Like many others, I was very influenced by Paramahansa Yogananda's book *Autobiography of a Yogi,* and so I took initiation into Kriya yoga, the form of *kundalini* yoga that he wrote so passionately about. As a result of the Kriya yoga meditation, I had powerful experiences of tremendous energy, light, and bliss. My first guru was an Indian swami who was a master of that system, and at the same time I was also under the tutelage of an American martial arts teacher. When I got involved with a teacher, I was completely committed and gave everything to what I was doing.

I was living in New York at the time and went to hear many different teachers speak. I was interested in everything—I went to see a Zen master, several different swamis, Tibetan lamas, a Sufi sheikh, a rabbi, and even Christian faith healers.

Were there any particular teachers among those you saw who had a big influence on you?

Yes. I heard a talk in a yoga center on Long Island by Swami Chidananda, President of the Divine Life Society and devoted disciple of the legendary Swami Sivananda. In the talk, which was about what it means to live the spiritual life, he said, "When someone asks you what you do, you should say: 'I MEDITATE! And... I also live.'" His outspoken and unequivocal declaration of the true priorities of a seeker had a very powerful impact on me.

Also, in 1980, I went to see J. Krishnamurti teach in Saanen, Switzerland. At this point in my life, I saw myself as being on the yogic path to liberation; I thought that I knew where I was going and how I was going to get there. Then I was told that there was a living Buddha named Krishnamurti who was going to die soon and that I should go hear him. When I arrived in Saanen, I went right to the tent where he was teaching—there were about two thousand people there—and I remember being struck by how beautiful he looked. The talk he gave was something along the lines of: Is it possible that thought is the source of all evil? I listened to the talk very closely but I could hardly understand anything that he said. At that time I just didn't have the background or enough experience to be able to comprehend what he was talking about. So whenever my mind wandered, I simply kept bringing my attention back to the sound of his voice because I had made up my mind that I wanted to pay attention to this man in any way that I could.

After the talk was over, I went back to my hotel room and lay down. When I got up, I noticed that something was different; something had changed. Suddenly, I realized that I was no longer so sure where I was going or how I was going to get there. In an undeniable yet mysterious way, something very important had happened through listening to this great man speak. He had somehow given me the freedom to question in a way that I never had before. I was thrilled to experience this unexpected space suddenly emerging within my mind. It's not that I felt that I had been on the wrong path but now there was room for real inquiry, a space within which to question that had not been there before.

Did you pursue any other kinds of spiritual practice?

Yes. At a certain point I began to go to Buddhist meditation courses, mainly because in that retreat environment I could meditate all day and night if I wanted to, for weeks at a time. The profound peace and intense clarity that resulted from such prolonged spiritual practice was very inspiring and the Buddha-dharma taught me a lot about the mind and how it works.

When I was twenty-seven, I went to India. The minute I arrived, I experienced a much greater freedom to give myself to my longing for liberation. Living in America, I had always felt inhibited, in one way or another, because so few seemed to share or even understand the intensity of my passion. In India, I found the confidence to abandon myself completely to the desire to become a liberated human being. I spent over two and a half years there, meditating and studying yoga. I also met my wife, who's Indian.

I know that you met your last teacher in India. How did that meeting take place?

A friend told me that there was a teacher still alive who was a direct disciple of Ramana Maharshi. He said that this teacher's name was H.W.L. Poonja, that he was a householder and very much like the great teacher of Advaita Vedanta, Nisargadatta Maharaj, who had recently died. Poonjaji was completely unknown at the time I went to see him. I had no great expectations because at that point I had been disillusioned in one way or another by all of my teachers. I wanted to "be a light unto myself," to be free of the burden of having to rely on anyone else.

I went to see Poonjaji for what I thought would be only three days. When I told him that I had no expectations, his response was, "That's good!" Then the next day, I asked him a question about making effort on the spiritual path and he replied: *"You don't have to make any effort to be free."* When he said that, something happened. For a split second, it became apparent to me that I had never been unfree. I *saw* it; I *knew* it. But then it was gone. And he smiled because he knew what had happened.

A few days later, I described to him, as I had to all my teachers, the experience of cosmic consciousness that had occurred when I was sixteen. To my surprise, he said, *"You knew everything then."* A powerful confidence in what had already happened began to emerge within me. It was miraculous. Something released and just let go. And I knew that my seeking had come to an end.

Over the next three weeks, there was an explosion inside me. Tremendous energy, experienced as overwhelming bliss, was so intense at times that I thought my body wouldn't be able to withstand it. I felt like I was going to explode into a thousand pieces. A powerful presence was slowly but surely consuming my entire being and I was scared at times. Day by day I was literally being overtaken by this conscious energy. Then, early one morning in a hotel room in Delhi, I sat up on my bed and heard the words come out of my mouth: "I surrender my life to You; do with me what You will."

After that I couldn't contain myself. When I went to meet with my friends, I would tell them about what had happened, about the glory of liberation here and now. And as I would speak to them, before my eyes they would be drawn into a state of meditation and would find themselves experiencing the same bliss that I was. They would feel with their own hearts and recognize with their own minds exactly what I was describing, *as* I was describing it. It was as if I was literally on fire and anybody who got too close to me started catching that same fire themselves.

When I went back to see Poonjaji, he said, "I knew this would happen—you're the one I've been waiting for my whole life and now that I've met you I can die." It was like a spiritual fairy tale. He also made it clear that he wanted me to be independent, not to rely on him in any way, because he felt—at least this is what he said to me at the time—that his work was over.

I went north and stayed in Rishikesh, a holy pilgrimage town on the Ganges River, with old and new friends. We spent day and night immersed in the bliss of Self-discovery, in the ecstasy and intimacy of knowing that there's only One

Self. That's when the teaching began. Soon I was invited to England, and many people started gathering around me. That was in 1986.

to cast no shadow 7

Q In your autobiography, you describe how you eventually parted ways with your last teacher. It seems that what started as a spiritual fairy tale didn't have a very happy ending.

A That's true. The fairy tale turned into a nightmare when it eventually became apparent that my teacher had more than one face. The agonizing ordeal I went through in trying to come to terms with the extreme split in his personality played a large part in initiating my ongoing quest to deeply understand what enlightenment actually is. Through his example and that of many other spiritual masters over the past few decades, it has become painfully clear that it is indeed possible for someone to go very far, to become a truly enlightened human being who is able to transmit the power and glory of this miraculous realization to others—and yet still be capable of behaving in ways that stand in stark contradiction to the absolute love that the experience of the True Self reveals.

Over time, I have come to understand that for radical spiritual transformation to be whole, not partial or incomplete, *two* things have to happen. One is the overwhelming experience of the grace and glory of the absolute dimension of life. The second is the purification of the vehicle—purification of the fundamental motives, conscious and unconscious, in the personality. Only then will we be truly fit to represent the glory of God without wanting even a small fraction of it for ourselves.

It sounds like you're saying that there are individuals who are enlightened in one sense but, because of impure motives, don't express a complete realization. You're saying that you have to be enlightened on both counts—

—to be the finished product, yes. Which means *whole*. Because unless the root of fundamental division in the personality has either been burned out by the blinding light of absolute love, or been deliberately relinquished through conscious surrender, enlightened consciousness itself can actually be used as an excuse for *not* being a living example of the very wholeness that we're speaking about. As strange as it sounds, when some people experience enlightened consciousness, it's not uncommon for them to conclude that now, because they are free, what they *do* doesn't matter. Some have even said things like: "What the personality says and what the body does is of no significance whatsoever—it's all an illusion anyway. The only thing that is real is the Self Absolute."

Ever since I began to seek for liberation, it has always seemed obvious to me that the overwhelming significance of the spiritual dimension of life only becomes apparent through the undeniable evidence of profound *human* trans-formation. That unborn, unseen reality must become mani-fest as you and I, so that this world that we're living in will literally be transformed by it. And the only way that can happen is if you and I become a living expression of that mystery and glory, that One without a second, *in this world.* One without a second means *undivided.* When there's only One without a second, then only one thing will be expressed, and that is Love.

The goal is to get to that point where the personality nat-urally and spontaneously expresses a perfect and seamless consistency of pure motivation. That means nothing is hid-den, there are no secrets, and nothing is personal. There's only One Self and in that One Self everything is known and everything is seen.

Do you think that the purification of the personality, the purifi-cation of the vehicle, is a process that's ever finished?

Well, it's definitely possible for a human being to get to a place where they are so naturally aligned with the spiritual dimension of life that they no longer have to make tremen-dous effort to resist marring its reflection in this world. But it's very rare. You know, in the end I think that ninety-nine percent of spiritual practice is about the purification of our motivation in relationship to the human experience. That means we make the noble effort to face and come to terms with the destructive nature of our petty self-concern in light of our true identity as One without a second. We face how much pride there is within us, how much aggression there is in our endless need to be someone special, how ultimately divisive is our desire to constantly see ourselves as being unique. When our interest in radical human transformation has been awakened, we begin to take ourselves on for everyone else's sake. We do whatever we have to do to come to a final reckoning with the darker motives inside ourselves, so that we will never again do anything in this world that would betray our passionate interest in being truly whole.

You see, when we get to that place, enlightened consciousness will be safe with us because then we won't do anything that would stain the reflection of its inherently perfect nature in the hearts and minds of an already cynical humanity. That's what it means to be a fit vehicle.

So are you saying that there are degrees of enlightenment?

Well, there are many different ways to answer that question. But one way is to say that there aren't degrees of enlightenment—there are only degrees of *un*enlightenment. In this way of looking at it, the degree to which ignorance falls away is the degree of enlightenment that there will be. When there is absolutely no ignorance left (if such a thing is possible!), you could say that someone is fully enlightened. So it would indeed appear that there are degrees of enlightenment but, in fact, it wouldn't be true.

There is a metaphor to describe this perspective. Imagine the radiant sun, forever burning brightly, always casting its immaculate light that is never touched by anything. Then imagine a mirror, the surface of which is completely covered with dry mud. This mirror cannot reflect the light of the sun because its surface is completely obscured. When you look at its surface all you will see is mud. Then something miraculous happens. A bolt of lightning hits the surface of the mirror and a small piece of the dry mud falls away. Now that mirror suddenly is casting a blazing reflection of the light of the radiant sun. Upon seeing this light, you instantly recognize it to be the light of your own Self. Then you see another mirror covered with mud but this one has been hit by *two* bolts of lightning and, as a result, a third of the surface of the mirror has been revealed. Now you say, "Oh my goodness! This light is *so* much brighter." And then you stumble upon a third mirror and this one has been struck by *three* bolts of lightning, revealing two-thirds of its surface, which is casting such a bright reflection of the light of the sun that your eyes can barely withstand its intensity. Eventually, you find a mirror that has been struck by so many lightning bolts that all of the mud has fallen away from its surface except for a few specks of dust. The reflection in this mirror is much, much brighter and clearer than all the others but those specks of dust still cast a small shadow. Then, finally, you find a mirror on which there is not even one speck of dust left. In this one there only is a perfectly pure and unobscured reflection of the radiant light of the sun.

The whole point is that the light shining on every one of those mirrors is the very same light. But final purity has been attained only when there's not even one speck of dust left to mar its reflection.

the ultimate challenge 8

Q *I have a question that relates very much to everything we've been discussing with regard to purity in spiritual teachers and also to the trials you have described on your own journey. My question is, how can we know when someone is fully enlightened or, in terms of the metaphor that you used, how can we know when the mirror is completely clean?*

A Well, if we really want to know the truth about others, we have to look very deeply into our own self. That means that with a ruthless integrity we must scrutinize our own motives and make the honest effort to find out what our relationship to life is *really* based on. Because in the end, our ability to determine another's purity of motivation and depth of spiritual attainment depends upon the purity of our *own* motives and the depth of our own attainment.

Why?

Because, simply put, spiritual evolution is a movement from a gross state of consciousness to one that is progressively more subtle and refined. And the gross cannot perceive the subtle. That means that we could find ourselves in the presence of an individual who was abiding in a state of consciousness that was infinitely more refined than our own but, because of the state of consciousness we were lost in, we would be unable to recognize their attainment.

If we really want to know the truth about enlightenment and find out where those who claim to be illumined actually stand in relationship to it, we need to find the strength of character to persistently scrutinize our own experience in light of their living example. Also, we need to spend as much time as possible in the company of those who *seem* to be abiding in that condition. And if we can do this, the answer to the important question you raised will slowly but surely begin to reveal itself. But—and this is the most challenging part of it— *you have to be ready for the answer.*

What does that mean?

It means that, one way or the other, it's probably going to be too much for you.

Why do you say that?

Well, if you find out that the teacher *is* authentic, you are in really big trouble—because then what are you going to do? Will you be able to handle the fact that living, breathing, enlightened consciousness is staring you right in the face, beckoning you to lose yourself forever in its majesty? Will you have the courage to surrender the fears and desires of your own ego in light of the blazing glory of the teacher's attainment?

Or if you discover, for one reason or another, that they're not authentic, that there is some impurity within them, what are you going to do then? Are you going to use their imperfection as an excuse to avoid facing the impure motives that are still very much alive within *you*? Will their failure empower your own devious ego and make it easy for you to turn your back on the call of your own Self and escape into cynicism?

I don't think I quite understand your point.

My point is that no matter where the teacher is at, in the end, it's always up to you to make sure that you don't compromise your own highest potential.

So are you saying it really doesn't matter where the teacher is at? That it's completely up to us?

Of course it matters where the teacher is at *and* it's completely up to you. This whole issue is more complicated than it may initially appear to be. You see, not all seekers are seeking for the same thing. In the name of "freedom" or "enlightenment," what many are looking for is not the challenge of a truly radical transformation but an easy escape from the turmoil and complexity of human life. They are looking for a powerful and charismatic person to save them, to relieve them of the burden of existence. They are definitely not looking for someone who will relentlessly face them with the ultimate challenge, never letting them compromise their own highest potential. They're not looking for someone to kill their ego! But ego death is the only true prize of the spiritual path and its pursuit is definitely not a game. In fact, it's the most all-demanding endeavor that a human being can embark on. You know, a lot of people say they want to be free but when they begin to find out what it really takes they usually change their minds pretty quickly, exclaiming, *"But I didn't know how big this was!"* Like the great J. Krishnamurti said, "If you knew what it was, you wouldn't touch it with a ten-foot pole."

I must admit, ego death doesn't sound very attractive to me.

That's my whole point. When most people find out how big this really is, they discover to their surprise that they're just not interested. And that's the most trying part of the task I'm endeavoring to accomplish—the fact that more often than not, when those who consider themselves to be sincere seekers come face to face with the demand to wholeheartedly embrace an absolute relationship to life here and now—which means to stop playing games and surrender the ego's agenda *for real*—they feel it's just too much.

As a teacher, that must put you in a difficult position.

Most definitely, it's very challenging. But the power in this teaching *is* that I am calling people to go all the way, to rise up to their own highest potential for the sake of something much greater than themselves. And as I've said, most people don't want to go that far. But I have no choice. You see, if a spiritual teacher is ever going to be able to effect a truly radical transformation in the lives of many others, they have to be bold, they have to be courageous, they have to have the audacity to follow the spiritual experience to its ultimate end. Because nothing will ever really change in this sleeping world, ever seduced and intoxicated by the fears and desires of the ego, unless someone is willing to say, "Yes, I am THAT and *I am willing to be responsible for it*." And when someone *is* willing to be responsible for it, they become an idealist, an impassioned idealist, and their very being forces a confrontation with the individual and collective ego. And if a spiritual teacher is actually embodying that kind of awakened inspiration, without their own ego usurping the inconceivably sacred nature of the endeavor, then they have become a powerful manifestation of enlightened consciousness unleashed in this world. As a surrendered soul, their only obligation is to ceaselessly, come what may, beckon any and all who have the eyes to see and the ears to hear to give themselves unconditionally to the call of their own spiritual heart. Why? *For everyone else's sake*, so that real revolutionary transformation can occur here and now in this world.

a straight line to the absolute   9

Q *You've made it clear that the path to freedom is a challenging one and that most people just aren't up for going all the way. If that is the case, where can I find the faith in myself to succeed where so many others have failed?*

A In the end, people "fail" only because of doubt or because they don't want it badly enough. In my own case, I had no doubt that it was possible to be free because I had had a very deep experience and I was convinced that sooner or later I was going to find it once again. And when I came to the conclusion that the liberating truth that I had glimpsed in that experience was more important than anything else—that life itself wouldn't make any sense without it—then the inspiration to take big risks and do whatever was necessary to succeed was never too far away.

It's for this reason that the foundation of my teaching is what I call "Clarity of Intention." Clarity of Intention is the irrevocable, unshakable commitment to attaining spiritual freedom, above all else, here and now, in this life. Being clear about one's intention to be free means one is ready and willing to do anything that one has to do in order to succeed.

So what does it actually mean to make this commitment?

Making this commitment means that we care about what's most important. It means we have come to the realization that unless we genuinely find a way to free ourselves from ignorance, it's going to be impossible to live a truly meaningful human life. It means we have looked with ruthless honesty at ourselves and discovered how deeply divided we are. And we have understood that as long as we remain divided in this way, our relationship to the world around us will inevitably be an expression of that division. You see, from the perspective of enlightenment, which means perfect wholeness, that fundamental division in the self is seen as the primary cause of all conflict. That is why an irrevocable, unshakable intention to be free of that division is the very foundation of the spiritual life.

"Irrevocable" is a pretty strong word.

It just doesn't work any other way.

Why not?

Because it's the irrevocable, undivided commitment to being free that literally aligns the separate sense of self with that which is absolute. You can experience this for yourself if you look directly into what it would mean to be completely free here and now. In order to do that you have to dare, if only for an instant, to let go of *everything*. This simply means to abandon any possibility in your own immediate experience that is not total unconditional freedom. If you can do this, the living presence of absolute singularity will begin to emerge in your awareness and the ego, or separate sense of self, will recoil in terror. "Oh, my God," it will say. "This is way too much!" That is because in the presence of that which is absolute, there is no room for a divided self to maneuver. And if you want to be free more than anything else, *that's the whole point.*

I can feel it as you speak about it.

Through the one-pointed contemplation of an unshakable commitment to being free here and now something powerful and deeply mysterious occurs: We find direct access to that which is absolute—*almost instantly.* So if we think that we want to be free, we should look into this question with utter sincerity, as if our life depended on it: What would it mean for me, whoever I think I am, to want to be free *more than anything else* right now, in this very moment and forever after? Through asking this one question, the whole world and everything in it begins to recede into the background. And something mysterious starts to happen. That's how powerful it is. I can also feel it now as I'm speaking about it. Simply through the contemplation of an unwavering commitment to being completely free, the whole world disappears and all I see is a straight line—a straight line to the Absolute. That's when we get a sense of how profound this question really is, because it's a line that takes us all the way there, *right now.*

So it actually is possible for most of us to be free?

Of course it is. It's just that most of us have not yet come to that point in our own evolution where we are willing to reach that high. The way it works is that as long as we are deeply invested in the ego, we will need to avoid at all costs the kind of unshakable commitment to being free that we've been speaking about. Why? Because *the commitment to being free means we will always only have one choice.* And the infinite space revealed by making that one choice is a suffocating place for the separate ego because it suddenly finds itself deprived of the whole world created by its endless fears and desires. That is why we will never *want* to be free more than anything else until we have reached that point in our own evolution where we are finally ready to give up the many for the One.

That's asking a lot!

I know. But the simple truth is that if you want to be truly free in this life, nothing less than everything will be enough. True freedom is an all-or-nothing deal. That's just the way it is—it's a spiritual law. But the good news is that if you're willing to pay the price, it *will* happen. Nothing will be able to stop it.

grace is not enough   10

Q *Andrew, you've spoken passionately about the power of the intention to be free, but isn't there another important aspect of all this, one that has nothing to do with choice, that some people call "grace"?*

A Yes. Grace is the spontaneous experience of a profound presence, in which there is no time but the consciousness of eternity, that is empty of self and full of ecstasy. And it is very important. But if we truly want to be free, the experience of grace is usually not enough. Over the years that I've been teaching, I've seen people become so completely overwhelmed by the descent of grace that they could barely contain the intensity of their joy and wonder and yet, in the end, it still wasn't enough to liberate them. The simple truth is that ecstasy and joy, awe and wonder are not, in and of themselves, enough to free any but the rarest of individuals from their own deeply conditioned minds. And it is because the conscious experience of divine presence usually grants us only a *temporary* respite from the ego's endless needs and concerns that that kind of experience, as inspiring as it may be, is just not enough to set us free.

If the experience of grace is usually only a temporary phenomenon, what can we do to make it more permanent?

That's simple. Ideally, when the miraculous presence of grace unexpectedly emerges from within and without—sweeping us off our feet, overwhelming us with ecstasy and a fearless confidence in our own true nature—we let go completely then and there, while we have the conviction to do so. That's the moment to surrender all the petty fears and desires of the ego once and for all—and never look back. But I said "ideally," and in the real world, most of us just aren't ready to surrender unconditionally even then. Therefore, to ensure that we succeed in this all-important endeavor, we have to become so doubtless about our own intention that our success or failure no longer depends upon the quality or the content of our experience. That simply means we stop waiting for anything at all to change before we will be finally ready to let go. You see, there are many things that we have no control over and the descent of grace is one of them. And because there is nothing we can do about it, we don't need to worry about it. If grace is going to descend upon us, it will. And if grace is not going to descend upon us, it won't. But our liberation need not depend on it. All we have to do is be willing to do *everything* that we possibly can to be free right now without holding back even a little. Then we are going to know what it means to go all the way and we are not going to have to wait for grace or anything else to pay us a visit. Of course, if it does, we'll be ready. But if not, we won't be waiting around.

The whole point is that if we truly want to be free here and now, we have to be willing to destroy the "meantime." The meantime is that eternity between now and that point in the future when we think we will be fully prepared to surrender unconditionally, finally ready to declare, "Not my will, but *Thy* will be done." If we are serious, the meantime is the most dangerous place to be because literally anything can happen in the meantime, including all kinds of wrong choices. If we allow ourselves to wait around for grace to descend, we will probably die in the meantime, not having made it. We will know that we are beginning to awaken for real when we recognize that there's absolutely nothing to wait for.

mere mortals   11

Q *You put a lot of emphasis on the role of choice on the path
to freedom. But what about those times when we're not
consciously choosing? There are periods when I feel like my life
is being guided, when I don't really feel like I'm the one who is
making the choices.*

A But that could never be completely true. Even if you
say that you are being guided in some way—and you very
well may be—*you* are still making the choice to allow that to
happen. As long as there is a human being who is walking
and talking, there is always going to be someone in there who
is making the choices. It doesn't matter who the person is or
how guided they may be. Even if an individual is free from
the small-minded and self-centered motives of ego, even if
their choices are the expression of a liberated heart and mind,
there is still an individuated self, no matter how transparent
it may have become, that exists, has preferences, and will
continue to make choices until the body drops. And in fact,
it is this very part of ourselves, the part that is making all the
choices, that we have to take responsibility for—that we have
to liberate from the ego—if we want to be free.

I find it paradoxical that when you're speaking about freedom you speak about responsibility at the same time.

Well, that's a big part of what spiritual freedom is all about—especially these days. Because in the end, our freedom doesn't depend upon whether we happen to *feel* free or "guided" or not—it depends upon what we choose to *do*. And as I have already said, the reason people are cynical about the concept of enlightenment is that too many of those who claimed to have attained this condition were apparently unwilling to take responsibility for what it is supposed to mean.

But isn't it difficult to take responsibility for being enlightened? I mean, many people look to you as an example. Do you ever feel burdened by that? By having to appear to be "perfect" in the eyes of those who believe in you?

What a question! Well, to be honest, no, I have never felt burdened by the need to appear in any particular way to others. But at times I am burdened by other people's unwillingness to wholeheartedly meet the very ideal that they claim to admire in me.

Well, isn't that an awful lot to expect from people?

That's my job—to expect a lot from people, to expect a lot more from them than they'd ever expect from themselves.

But aren't we all only human? I mean, if we're not enlightened yet, there's only so much we mere mortals can do.

Mere mortals? I'm a mortal just like you. Don't push me away, don't make me unreachable. I'm a human being made of flesh and blood, just like you. Everything that I'm speaking about, anybody can realize, if they take it seriously enough. It's far too easy to say, "It's not possible for me, but *you can do it because you're special.*" Don't you see—that's how you let yourself off the hook. The belief that "I already know that it's not possible" is just cynicism. And cynicism is just pride. It's just ego. If you do want to be free then that's the very part of yourself that you have to let go of.

Are you saying that the belief that it's not possible comes from the ego?

Yes, of course. The ego protects itself from its own potential destruction through convincing us that it "already knows" that it's not possible to be free. Because freedom means its own death. That's why the ego endlessly takes refuge in the cynical position of "already knowing." You see, if we already know that it's not possible, then there's no need to take any risks or to be vulnerable in any way. But when we dare to make room for the unthinkable possibility of our own liberation, we have to allow ourselves to be vulnerable, which simply means to not be so sure, to *not* know. It's only when we are willing to really not know that we may discover, to our own astonishment, that it actually is possible.

It's not that I don't want to believe it's possible. But there's a fear—

That's because underneath the cynical idea that it's not possible you're afraid that it may actually *be* possible. That's how it always is. Underneath the cynicism is fear of ego death. Everybody wants to get enlightened but nobody wants to change.

I suppose that's true.

The great challenge of enlightenment, for all of us mere mortals, is radical transformation. It's the demand to come to a final reckoning with the enormity of what it means to be alive. Some people wait until they are on their deathbed to do this; most manage to avoid it completely. If we want to be free, we want to come to this final reckoning *now* while we still have time left.

Time to do what?

To defy the cynical ego. To transcend it and prove that it's possible to become an example of pure motivation. To live the law of love in a deeply divided world. Unless some of us are willing to do this, no one is ever going to believe that it's possible.

the end of karma   12

Q   *Andrew, I find the ideal you're pointing to very inspiring.
But it's far from my own experience. You know, I still do things I re-
gret—act out of unconscious patterns in ways that hurt other people.*

A   Then I guess you must still be creating lots of karma!

What do you mean by that?

Well, we create karma when we act out of ignorance and selfishness in ways that cause suffering to others. For most of us,
a long history of countless selfish actions has created a powerful momentum that is very difficult to break. That momentum is what karma is. And breaking the momentum of karma
is what enlightenment is all about.

But isn't there such a thing as "good" karma?

Of course there is—but that's not the kind you have to worry
about! If you want to be free, liberating yourself from the
destructive momentum of bad karma is *all* you need to be
concerned with.

So when you say that we create bad karma through acting out of ignorance and selfishness, what exactly does that mean? Does that include thinking? In other words, do we cause suffering to people around us if we think negative thoughts?

Yes, you're killing me! Just kidding. No, in my teaching, the only way karma is created is through *action*—not mere thinking, but an action in time and space that expresses self-concern at the expense of others.

So does that mean that I can indulge in hours and hours of selfish thinking and then have no problem going out into the world and acting generously?

Well, if you're crazy enough to spend hours and hours lost in selfish thinking, obviously you're deeply identified with those thoughts, and therefore, it is very unlikely that you wouldn't act out of at least some of them. You see, whenever we *identify* with the content of thought, that *is* an action, and that action can and will have real consequences in the world. If you want to be free, you will not want to identify with those thoughts that express ignorance and selfishness and, because of that simple fact, no karma will be created and there will be no negative consequences in the world.

I still have a question about that. For example, I believe that this plant here is sensitive to what I'm thinking. I believe that I could sit here very quietly, appearing to do nothing at all, but at the same time have thoughts of hurting this plant and it would suffer.

Maybe it would; maybe it wouldn't.

There have been experiments that show that the thoughts we have about animals and plants affect them. They are extremely sensitive. So therefore you could say that thoughts actually are kinds of actions.

It's not that simple. You see, if you believe that the mere presence of any particular thought has *inherent* power, it will. But the door to liberation is found when you discover that the mere presence of thought has no power whatsoever *unless you believe that it does.* So, if you are looking at a plant and are strongly identified with a negative thought about it, something negative will be transmitted. But if you are not identified with that negative thought, it will have no power to transmit anything. Remember, it is only your *relationship* to thought and the content of thought that either gives it power or strips that power away. And it is through your own recognition of this profoundly liberating truth that you will find the way to break the momentum of karma and experience the extraordinary wholeness of being that this discovery makes possible.

I can feel the liberation in what you're saying but for some reason it's hard for me to accept.

That's because, like most seekers, you're superstitious. "Superstitious" means that you are convinced that the mere presence of thought *automatically* means something about the thinker. And as a result, you can't help but be living in constant fear of your own mind. Don't you see, that's the definition of bondage. And that's why, if you really want to be free, seeing clearly that *thought has no power except that which we choose to give it* is so, so important.

So are you saying that if we want to be free, we just don't identify with any thoughts?

No, I'm not saying that. As long as we are human beings who are living in the real world, we have to have a relationship with thought. Why? Because we have to *act*. Because we have to make choices. That can't be avoided. And that is why, if we want to be free, the big question isn't, "How do I *not* identify with thought?" but, more importantly, "What is the *right* relationship with thought?"

So what is the right relationship with thought?

The right relationship with thought is one in which we identify only with those thoughts that are in line with our desire to be free.

That's quite a tall order!

Yes, it is. But remember, the goal of the spiritual path is enlightenment and that's not a small matter. One definition of enlightenment is that one has come to that point in one's own evolution where one is no longer creating karma. That means that one is no longer acting out of ignorance or selfishness in ways that cause suffering to others. And in the end, this simple yet profound attainment is entirely dependent upon one's relationship with thought.

true conscience   13

Q   What is the role of awareness on the spiritual path? In
light of everything you've been saying about the importance of
making the right choices if we want to be free, how can we learn
to be more attentive?

A   Well, if you truly want to be free, you *will* be aware,
you will be paying attention. You see, there are different
kinds of awareness. One kind of awareness is where you,
whoever you are, are consciously making effort to be aware
of everything that you are doing. But there is another kind
of awareness that is more mysterious. And you will begin
to discover this mysterious awareness as you surrender
more and more to your own desire to be free. At times
there will be an unexpected movement from deep within
you; a response will arise that moves faster than thought.
You will do something or say something that expresses
the passionate intensity of enlightened consciousness—
a consciousness that, a moment before, you had no awareness of. You will have the strange sense of not knowing
who responded, even though it was none other than your
own Self.

Experiences like this reveal to us beyond any doubt that our True Self is always paying attention in a way that we are usually not conscious of. And when we discover *this* Self—this mysterious depth that is already awake—we find that which is miraculous. We discover who we truly are. It's the Self that we cannot see with the mind, but when we experience it directly we will understand what it means to be enlightened. And when we liberate this Self that mysteriously sees and knows what we cannot see or know with our conscious mind, we will begin to respond to life in ways that, left to our own devices, we never could.

Are you saying that we can be aware without even knowing it?

Yes. If we are true to the desire to be free, we will find that we always *are* paying attention, even at times when, in our conscious experience, it appears to us that we are not. This happens to me often in my own life. Sometimes my own inner experience may appear to be, for a certain period of time, quite mundane. And then a response will occur to some event that is happening around me, a response that is so fast and so precise that it amazes me every time. I don't know where it comes from. I only become aware of it *as* it's happening. In retrospect, I see that I was responding to something that I wasn't even aware of. But obviously, a part of me was paying attention all the time, a part that "I," Andrew, the individual self, wasn't conscious of. So we have to ask, "Who is it really that is paying attention? Who is it that is aware?"

So when you speak about paying attention, you're referring to something quite mysterious.

Usually when we speak about paying attention, we are only referring to that which engages the conscious mind. The problem is that it leaves the most important part of our self out of the picture, which is that part of our self that we can *never* know with the conscious mind. This is an extraordinary secret that not very many people know about. But that's what enlightenment is—it is the liberating discovery of the profound mystery of our own Self, a mystery that we will never be able to understand with the mind.

Can you say more about this mystery?

Well, this is very difficult to appreciate without direct experience but the most important part of this mystery is the revelation of what I call "true conscience."

Which is?

The unexpected manifestation of intense compassion. True conscience emerges from that very same mysterious part of our own self; it expresses a kind of care that the personality could never understand. It's the true heart, which is *not* the heart that we normally identify with the personality. It's the heart that breaks when we directly experience the One Self that we are when we have no notion of being separate. This true conscience, or this spiritual conscience, is experienced as *caring*. And this caring is painful—a painful emotional experience—but it's this caring that finally liberates us, slowly but surely, from the attachment to the ego and its endless fears and desires. It is the emergence of this conscience that gives us the energy, strength, and inspiration to give ourselves to the most important task that there is.

So if we want to be free, it's very important to ask ourselves: How much do I care? Because when our heart breaks in the way that I've been describing, we will, maybe for the very first time in our lives, experience a liberating distance from self-concern. Suddenly we will find that we are consumed by that mystery and we will spontaneously begin to express a passion for that which is sacred. It's only then that everything will begin to make sense.

Is the conscience that you've been speaking about another word for love?

Yes. The degree to which we are able to liberate ourselves from self-concern will be the degree to which we are able to recognize that our true nature as human beings is love. It happens automatically. This is one of the miracles of human life. When you have reached that point in your own evolution when you are ready to leave self-concern behind, your heart will expand and you will know a love that is impossible to imagine unless you have experienced it for yourself. The nature of this love is not personal; it does not have its roots in the personality. When our attention has become liberated from self-concern, this conscience is set free. Love is literally liberated from the depths of our own being and just emerges of its own accord—even forcefully at times.

It is so inspiring when one directly experiences the miracle that lies beyond self-concern. The discovery of true conscience instills in us such a profound faith in the very essence of life itself. And anybody can know this miracle if they really want to. They just have to be willing to pay the price.

the only obstacle   14

Q   *Andrew, throughout our conversation you've referred to the ego several times. Could you explain what your definition of "ego" is?*

A   Yes, I'd be happy to. Ego is the one and only obstacle to enlightenment. Ego is pride. Ego is arrogant self-importance. Ego is the deeply mechanical and profoundly compulsive need to *always* see the personal self as being separate from others, separate from the world, separate from the whole universe. Ego is a love-denying obsession with separation, narcissism, and self-concern.

Wow! Aren't you making the ego into a bit of a demon?

Well, from the perspective of enlightenment, it *is*.

But isn't there another way to look at the ego?

Yes, of course there is. My definition is strictly from the per-spective of enlightenment. When psychologists speak about the ego, they are referring to something else altogether. To speak in broad generalities, the psychological definition of ego refers to what could be called a "self-organizing principle" in the psyche. It is a psychological function that organizes the different elements of the self in order to create some semblance of wholeness and integration. If *this* function is not in good working order, we are going to be in bad shape.

So when you use the word "ego," you're referring to something completely different?

Yes. When teachers of enlightenment use the word "ego," they are referring very specifically to that emotional and psychological knot in consciousness that is the fundamental cause of the sense of separation from all of life. Once again, from the spiritual perspective, this is defined as pride, self-importance, and the narcissistic need to *always* see oneself as being separate.

And in order to be free, we have to liberate the self from that need?

Yes, exactly. Drop it like a hot potato!

Do you mean all at once, just like that?

If we truly want to be free, we can't do it fast enough.

But don't you think that most of us need some time to understand what it is that we're trying to let go of in the first place? Wouldn't it make it easier to transcend the ego if we first did some kind of psychological work—work that would help us understand ourselves and the causes of the pain associated with our past?

Well, that's like saying, "Before I take a bath and get really clean, I think I'll jump into the garbage can and have a look around"!

You see, when someone says, "I want to be free," that means free from the never-ending fears and desires of the separate ego. Choosing to spend hours and hours in a process of intense identification with those fears and desires in the name of eventually transcending them doesn't even make logical sense. If we're sincere in our desire to be free, then letting go of the fears and desires of the ego always means *now*. That's the whole point anyway. We'll never be free any other way. As long as we believe there is some value in closely examining the contents of the garbage can of the ego's endless woes, then it simply means that we have not yet realized that it's all only dirty garbage. So until that moment in time when we have glimpsed the enlightened perspective for ourselves and witnessed the unreality of the ego and its personal agenda, the answer to your question would have to be "yes." But it would only be because you had not yet seen the liberating truth for yourself. You had not yet seen the ego, with its masquerade of self-importance and its never-ending agenda, for what it really is: empty and ultimately meaningless, only a source of painful enslavement to a world of illusion and falsehood.

As long as we believe, in our unenlightenment, that there's something of value to be found there, we will continue to insist, "I *know* how bad it smells, I really do, and I also know that my clothes will get terribly stained and I'll need to take a bath when I'm finished, but I *have* to go in there. It's *very* important!" You see, as long as we are fundamentally identified with the separate sense of self, there will be a deep conviction inside us that its never-ending agenda really matters. Why? "Because it's *me*."

So as long as you are identifying with the garbage, you are the ego and, as long as this is happening, that means that you can't transcend it—right?

Yes, that's right.

But again, in order to not identify with the garbage of the ego, don't you have to look into it in some way first?

No. In fact, it is only when we take the enormous risk of *not* looking into it, of leaving the ego *completely alone,* that we will finally be able to see it for what it really is. It takes tremendous courage to do this. Again, if you want to see the ego *objectively,* you have to leave it completely alone. There's no other way to achieve the liberating result that I'm speaking about. It's an all-or-nothing game and most people don't want to play because the stakes are just too high.

What's so challenging about this is the unconditional nature of enlightenment itself. You see, we are speaking about a leap beyond time into another dimension that reveals a perspective that is absolute. That perspective will simply not acknowledge the reality of the world that the ego lives in—because within that absolute perspective, the ego just does not exist. That's why I was saying it's an all-or-nothing game. If you want to know what that perspective is for yourself, you have to be willing to leave this one behind. It's leaving one world behind and entering into another; it's discovering a completely different way of seeing. The ego will *never* do this. Even the sensitive, intelligent ego will insist that the garbage is important. Of course, it will have enough perspective to recognize that it's pretty smelly and not so wholesome, but in the end its own survival depends upon clinging to the unquestioned conviction that it is important.

So in the enlightened perspective, there is a non-relative or absolute shift in the way that we see and it's in that shift that the recognition occurs that it is indeed *all* garbage. And from the point of view of the separate ego and personal self, this absolute position will *always* appear to be way too much. It will be seen as being too extreme. And of course, the truth is that it *is*. The enlightened perspective, because of its non-relative or absolute nature, will always be seen as way too much from any position that insists on reducing *everything* to that which is merely relative.

So you can see why I would never be able to say "yes" to the question you're asking and be the kind of teacher that I am. From my point of view, and from the kind of liberation teaching that I'm trying to share with people, I would never be able to say "yes." *As long as we still believe that there's any relevance to what's in that garbage can, there will never be any real freedom.* Because every moment that we insist on looking at our experience from a context that is merely relative, like it or not, we will be feeding, empowering, giving reality to the only part of ourselves that's keeping us all in hell.

Andrew, everything you're saying seems to make sense, but why do I still feel so strongly that I need more time, that I'm not ready to let go yet?

Because the ego *always* needs more time. The perennial refrain of the ego in the face of the call from the Absolute is, "I'm not ready yet, I need more time." And it always sounds so reasonable—from a relative perspective. But from an absolute perspective *there is no time.* And the call of the spirit, the call of the True Self—the command to evolve to a higher state of consciousness—comes from that absolute dimension where time does not exist. Once again, the Absolute never hears the ego's pleas. Its ceaseless refrain is: "Every moment that you hesitate, you're keeping yourself from me." Its constant demand is always, *"Now!"* and the ego insists, yet again, "No, I'm not ready." This is the spiritual drama that has played itself out between man and God for thousands of years—between the individual sense of self and the call of the Absolute. The whole point of spiritual life is to surrender unconditionally to that call, and that means the end of time—the end of *your* time. This is what the spiritual drama is all about—the dynamic tension between the ego's endless excuses and the call for unconditional submission from the Absolute.

liberation beyond gender 15

Q You've just been speaking about the ego and the challenges we face on the path to liberation. What do you think about the idea that these challenges are different for men and for women? Is the path fundamentally the same for both sexes or should there be different paths?

A Assuming that the goal is enlightenment, there is only one path. Of course, there *are* fundamental differences between men and women and, if we want to be free, these traits need to be acknowledged and deeply understood. But once again, if the goal is our own perfect liberation here and now, what is important is *not* the fact that these differences exist, but our unconditional willingness to face them totally and in such a way that they could never be an obstacle to that goal. However, if the spiritual path we're pursuing is not about total liberation, which means the transcendence of all differences, but rather is about embracing our differences in the form of gender consciousness in a deeper and more authentic way, then of course the path will be different for men and women—as will be its goal. And in this case, it will be the very notion of difference and the spiritual significance of that difference, that will define what the path is all about.

But even if the goal is the same, as men and women, don't we have different obstacles to overcome?

On a superficial level, yes, but when we're speaking about transcending the ego and leaping beyond the known, all human beings have to pay the same price. Any spiritual path that puts too much emphasis on notions of difference is bound to inadvertently strengthen the ego or separate sense of self. Of course, it may be tempting to become fascinated with these relative differences but, in doing so, we quickly lose sight of the goal, which is freedom from *any* fixed notion of self.

So in relationship to gender, what does it mean to be free from any "fixed" notion of self?

It means that our True Self *is* free from any notion of gender, free from any sense of difference whatsoever. And in order to discover that Self, which is our "natural state" or already liberated condition, the intense attachment to and identification with being a separate personality, including its maleness or femaleness, has to be transcended.

But what about the reality of the body? What about the fact that we are men and women and these gender differences actually do exist? Does wanting to be free mean that we have to deny these differences?

No, not at all. If we want to be free, we have to surrender our emotional and psychological *investment* in being male or female, not the reality of the fact that our body is male or female. Because if we deny anything that's real or true, we'll never be free. The goal, as I was saying, is to discover the natural state. In this case, the natural state means free from ego. Free from ego means free from the emotional and psychological investment that creates self-consciousness. So in relationship to the whole notion of gender, what do you think the liberated or natural expression of our maleness or femaleness would look like?

I don't know. But I imagine it would look pretty good.

It would be *unself-conscious*—which means free from our usual not-so-subtle narcissistic identification with our gender.

And without self-consciousness, what would the differences look like?

Well, if we want to be free, that's exactly what we want to find out for ourselves. We want to discover in every moment what the egoless, which means unself-conscious, expression of gender actually looks like.

But can you tell me what you think it would look like?

It would look *innocent*. That means that our gender con-sciousness would be free from the ego's unsavory motives—

free from the need to dominate, control, and seduce. What do you think this world would be like if we never used our gender differences to affirm the separate ego? What would our relationships be like, as men and women, if we ceased to use our gender differences to wield power over each other? If you think about it, you'll begin to see that the implications of what I'm pointing to are revolutionary.

I can't even imagine a world like that.

the promise of perfection   16

Q *Andrew, at the end of our discussion of gender, you brought up an issue that is obviously very important to a lot of people—relationships. So I wanted to ask you about your view on this: Do you think it is possible to be free within a romantic relationship?*

A Almost impossible! The sexual/romantic experience is one of the most confusing areas of human life and seems to be the hardest to get clear about. You see, the sexual/romantic experience almost always creates profound attachment—deep emotional and psychological attachment. And the problem is that if we want to be free, that is the very thing we want to liberate ourselves from.

But you're married, aren't you?

Yes, I have been for many years.

So isn't it possible to pursue freedom together? Can't we walk the path to enlightenment in the context of a sexual/romantic relationship?

One would hope so—but the way you're asking the question, because it implies a fear of losing something, points to exactly what the problem is. Once again, the thing about sex and romance is that it creates powerful attachment. That is its nature. It is not a free ride—unfortunately. And, therefore, unless we get our priorities clear, it's almost inevitable that that attachment will quickly become more important to us than our own potential liberation in this life. I hear so many people say, "We want to pursue freedom *together*," but what that almost always means is that holding on to the intensely personal experience of sentimental attachment is their first priority—*not* the experience of profound inner freedom.

But I don't understand why there has to be a conflict between freedom and being together.

Well, it depends what you mean by freedom. From the perspective of enlightenment, to be free means to be *free from attachment*. Attachment means, "I *have* something." But to be free means, "I have *nothing*." You see, when you hold on to absolutely nothing, you are free—automatically. And the truth that liberates is the profound recognition of just that fact—*that your own natural state is already free*. The only thing that keeps us in bondage is the unquestioned belief that there is something fundamental that is missing from our own self. So out of ignorance of our own natural state, we bind ourselves to people and things, convinced that through creating attachment we will find happiness and content-ment. But it never works that way. Because where there is attachment, there is always fear of loss. And where there is fear, there can never be real happiness or deep contentment. It is the revelation of enlightenment itself that shows all of this directly to us—the perennial truth that real happiness and the only lasting contentment lie within us as our own True Self, our own natural state, already full and complete as it is. But in this unenlightened world, we are all deeply conditioned to believe that happiness and contentment lie somewhere outside our own self. If we truly want to be free, we renounce that way of thinking. We give it up because we have had intimations of a profound happiness that is already present deep within our own self, a lasting contentment that will be ours only when we finally stop looking for it anywhere else.

I do feel strongly drawn toward the profound freedom you're describing but I also feel like it's a natural thing to want to be in a relationship. From the way you're speaking, it almost sounds like you're advocating celibacy.

Is that what I said?

Well, not specifically...

So many people tend to misinterpret what I am saying whenever I speak about this particular topic. It's very revealing. This is such a loaded issue for most of us. And as I said earlier, it's *very* difficult to see clearly into this area of the human experience, especially when it relates to ourselves. All I'm trying to do is present the facts. You asked about sex, romance, and enlightenment, and all I'm saying is that the definition of spiritual freedom is *freedom from attachment*. Sex creates attachment—that's all there is to it. And that is why there is almost always an inherent conflict between the longing for inner freedom and the karmic consequences of the sexual/romantic experience. Therefore, the big question is: If enlightened freedom is freedom from attachment, then what are we all going to do about the relentless nature of sexual attraction?

I was hoping you were going to give me an answer to that one!

Well, there have been widely differing answers to this perennial question that have been offered to men and women throughout the ages. On one extreme, we have been encouraged to use the sexual experience itself as a vehicle for self-transcendence and, on the other, we have been told that if we want to be liberated men and women, we have to renounce the sexual experience altogether. I believe that if we want to be free, we must think very deeply about these matters for ourselves. We can't naïvely assume that there is a simple, ready-made answer to such a complex and loaded question. And if we are sincere, we have to be willing to bear the burden of that complexity on our own shoulders and figure it out for ourselves. If even enlightened masters have come to such contradictory conclusions about this fundamental issue, then it just points us back to ourselves and our own honest inquiry into one of life's most challenging questions.

But have you come up with an answer?

I don't want to answer the question for you. If you want to be free, then all you need to know is that free means *free from attachment*. That simple fact transcends the relative matter of whether you're in a relationship or not in a relationship. If you face that spiritual truth unflinchingly, then you will be looking into the heart of the matter for yourself. And that takes a lot more courage than blindly accepting someone else's conclusions.

So then what does it mean to give up attachment?

It means recognizing for ourselves that the *promise* of perfect happiness and blissful fulfillment inherent in sexual desire is overwhelmingly deceptive. It means that we are very clear about the difference between the personal bliss of the romantic interlude and the impersonal ecstasy of spiritual freedom. It means that we choose to renounce personal affirmation for the ecstatic contentment that emerges spontaneously when we finally stop looking outside our own self for the experience of completion. But realistically, in a world like ours that is incessantly propagating this powerful promise, if we want to be free, we all, to some degree at least, have to be willing to be renunciates!

What do you mean by being a renunciate?

In this context, renunciation means resisting the temptation to be seduced by the most powerful illusion that there is.

And that illusion is?

It's what I call "the promise of perfection." It says: "If I follow this impulse to its ultimate conclusion, I'm going to find perfect happiness and total contentment—I will experience a deep sense of wholeness; I will finally be complete." We do this over and over again and continue to miss the simple truth that the bliss we experience in the romantic interlude never lasts and ultimately creates painful attachment. And also, it is only when we let go of the promise of perfection that it will become clear to us how, more often than not, the experience of romantic intoxication is fueled by the ego's need for personal affirmation.

Okay, okay ... where's the nearest monastery?! But seriously, Andrew, if what you're saying is true, would there be any reason left to be in a relationship? Even though it's obviously not what you mean, it still keeps sounding like you're saying that if we want to be free, we have to give up the whole thing.

Well, yes and no. Yes, if it means creating more suffocating attachment that only serves to perpetuate the illusory personal world of the separate ego. But no, if the context for personal intimacy and sexual communion is authentic spiritual freedom.

What does that mean?

It means that we want to be free more than anything else and therefore are more interested in impersonal ecstasy than personal bliss. It means that the context for personal intimacy and sexual communion would be the *impersonal*—a dimension that is unknown in this world, that is beyond ego and free from attachment.

And where is this impersonal dimension found?

Inside your own self. When you renounce the endless self-centered concerns of the separate ego and its small personal perspective, then spontaneously you will find yourself there. That is where you will discover an absolute love, a bliss that is empty of attachment and free from the conviction that anything fundamental is missing. And it is that context alone, which is one of inherent fullness or completion, that can make it possible for human beings to come together in personal intimacy and sexual communion in a way that is free from the pain, complexity, and unending confusion that are usually such an inherent part of this area of life.

an unbroken universal unfolding 17

Q *One of the fundamental components of your teaching is what I believe you call "the impersonal view." Could you explain what you mean by this?*

A Yes. What I call "the impersonal view" is what the enlightened perspective actually is. From the enlightened perspective there is only *one* human experience and that one human experience is recognized to be an impersonal affair, a *universal* unfolding. The impersonal view always sees through and beyond that which is merely personal. A perspective that is merely personal traps us forever in the deeply painful and never-ending melodrama of the separate self and inherently limits our ability to see beyond the illusion of independent self-existence. From the enlightened perspective, we see that it is the deeply conditioned, profoundly mechanical habit of *personalization* that creates ego, the psychological and emotional barrier that separates us from our own Self and the rest of life in every moment. That is why making the effort to see beyond a perspective that is merely personal is essential if we want to be free.

So how can we discover this impersonal perspective for ourselves?

By paying attention to our own experience in an honest way. Without being aware of it, we personalize almost every movement of thought and feeling. Every single experience we have, from the gross to the subtle, we compulsively call *"mine."* Yet if we stand back even a little, we will quickly discover that so much of what we experience is not unique or personal in any way. Think about it. Look and see how much of our shared human experience is exactly the same, and yet how, through the deeply ingrained habit of personalization, we compulsively create the appearance of difference—the very illusion that is the sole cause of all of our unnecessary suffering. You see, in the impersonal view, which is the enlightened perspective, the ego and the entire personal world that it creates is not seen as being real. That world is revealed to be empty of meaning, value, and purpose, ultimately serving only to perpetuate the existence of a separate self that doesn't really exist.

What do you mean when you say it doesn't really exist?

When you discover who you really are, you see directly that the personal self, with its attachment to time and history, lives in a dream world, an unending nightmare of countless worries and fears, desires and hopes, which literally become transparent when one awakens to one's own impersonal absolute depth. And when that impersonal Self Absolute begins to emerge in consciousness as a living presence, the "personal," instead of being the impenetrable fortress that the separate ego abides in, becomes a permeable vessel through which the impersonal Self Absolute seeps into this world.

So what you're saying is that the "Self Absolute" is impersonal and it is that self that begins to shine through in the enlightened state. What happens to the old personality then? What happens to the personal self?

It becomes liberated! And that liberation is a result of directly seeing, again and again and again, the ultimately impersonal nature of the apparently *personal* dimension of the human experience, including all its unique twists and turns and endless variations.

So from the perspective you're describing, you're saying there's really nothing personal in either the absolute or the relative dimension of our experience.

That's exactly what I'm saying. The personal dimension, from a personal perspective, will be seen as being *personal*. But that same personal dimension, from an impersonal perspective, will be seen as being *impersonal*. The whole point is that our relationship to our experience depends upon how we see it, how we *interpret* it. So the important question is: Are we still compulsively personalizing all of our experience? Does the way we interpret our experience have anything at all to do with the impersonal view? Because remember, the enlightened perspective always points us to that which is singular, empty of anything personal, and free from any and all motivation that comes from ego. Therefore, if we want to be free, the terrifying yet liberating truth of impersonality cannot be escaped. Sooner or later, we must summon up the courage to face directly into the ultimately impersonal nature of our very own personal experience. Because you see, the truth is that we really are all in the same boat, on the same sea, going to the same destination. The problem with a perspective that is fundamentally personal is that it makes it impossible to know this. It makes it impossible to see beyond our own ego to enlightened freedom itself, where we discover a truth that is universal, absolute, and definitely not personal.

I am beginning to sense the truth of what you are pointing to, but it makes my head spin! I feel like I don't know who or what I am ...

That's what happens. And if you stay with this inquiry, you will end up at a place inside your own self where there is absolute singularity—where the personal becomes the impersonal and the impersonal becomes the personal. In that place, it is literally impossible to distinguish between the two.

But why is that?

Because there is only one Self and there is only one human experience. That's liberation. But to discover this for yourself, you have to take the inquiry all the way to the end. A merely superficial effort will never get you there. That place of absolute singularity is where true freedom and enlightened understanding are found. That is where the relative and the Absolute, the personal and the impersonal, merge and become one. In that mysterious place, they become one unbroken universal unfolding that is free from the bondage of duality.

impersonal enlightenment 18

Q *When you were just speaking about the impersonal view, I felt the power of seeing beyond the personal. It was almost as if my individual sense of self became diffused and I experienced the kind of transparency you described.*

A That's good—beginning to awaken to emptiness or transparency, seeing through the personal dimension of our own experience, directly realizing that it is not "my experience" but the *human experience*. That's the first step. But there's a lot more. Because when we become deeply established in that realization something unexpected begins to emerge in our awareness. Something that we were not looking for. It is the recognition of an enormous responsibility, a responsibility that is now ours simply because we have seen through the illusion of the personal. In fact, with the realization of impersonality, we suddenly experience in a mysterious way that the evolutionary potential of the human race rests on our very own shoulders. As overwhelming as it sounds, it's actually true. And even this is impersonal, because whenever spiritual awakening is genuine, this sense of an obligation to life itself is experienced in a way that is direct and profound. In this radical awakening beyond the personal—which I call "Impersonal Enlightenment"—the burden of the as-yet-unfulfilled promise of human evolutionary potential is felt directly and very *personally*.

Wait a minute! How did we get from recognizing that most of what we experience is impersonal to discovering that the burden of human evolution is resting on our own shoulders?

Well, that's the way it works. It's just that few seekers get far enough to experience this directly for themselves. But if you do finally transcend the need to compulsively personalize all of your experience, this mysterious sense of obligation to an evolutionary imperative will begin to reveal itself spontaneously. It is then that you will discover what J. Krishnamurti was pointing to when he said, "*You* are the world." That's when you recognize yourself to be the human condition *as a whole*. And in that recognition, you automatically feel responsible for that condition because you are simply feeling responsible for your own self. It is just an inherent part of the realization that I'm speaking about—the realization of impersonal enlightenment.

So are you saying that I should try to feel more responsible for the evolution of the rest of the human race?

No. All I'm saying is that when your fascination with the fears and desires of your own ego burns away for real, when you experience that miraculous leap beyond the personal, to your surprise, what will begin to emerge within you is a deep and profound caring for your own Self, which *is* all of us.

Can you describe what this feels like in your own experience?

Yes. There is a passion that arises from deep within—and I can honestly only describe it as a command from the unknown—that at times becomes an overwhelming roar. It is a power and a presence that feels infinitely conscious, a vast intelligence that is not personal in any way. And I know that until the day I die, it will never be satisfied. It can't, because until every human being has awakened, indeed, until each of us has reached our full evolutionary potential, it will not be enough. And of course, that's not going to happen—at least not anytime soon. But this passion is simply an expression of the awakened state. It is the evolutionary imperative becoming manifest. And it is totally impersonal and utterly choiceless. It's what the experience of impersonal enlightenment is all about.

What you are describing is compelling. But it's nothing like I've imagined freedom to be. Being inspired by a passion that will never be satisfied almost sounds more like a kind of bondage.

It is! But that's the whole point—it's what I call *the bondage of liberation,* the bondage of liberation beyond the personal. You see, in impersonal enlightenment, the ultimate goal is not one's own liberation but the liberation of everyone else. It is not merely the attainment of personal freedom, which I call personal enlightenment. Of course, profound freedom, ecstatic joy, and deep contentment *are* the by-product of a life lived in service of the evolutionary imperative, but they are definitely not the goal of impersonal enlightenment.

the complete picture 19

Q *Andrew, it's clear that in your view, enlightenment, or what you call "impersonal enlightenment," is about changing this world, literally transforming it. But I've heard other teachers describe enlightenment as the opposite of that—as the end of trying to change anything.*

A Well, actually, *both* are true. And it is this paradoxical fact that makes what enlightenment is, and what it really means, so difficult for many seekers—and also a lot of teachers—to grasp. There are two fundamental components of the experience of enlightenment. Simply put, one is the liberating revelation that *everything is always perfect as it is*—at all times, in all places, under all circumstances. In this, there is a profound letting go of fear and attachment. The other component is what I've been calling the evolutionary imperative, which is activated by spiritual awakening. It is experienced as a powerful demand for evolution and transformation here and now for the sake of life itself. This apparent paradox—that everything is already perfect *and* everything must change—is the complete picture of what enlightenment is all about.

But how could both be true? What you're describing sounds to me like a complete contradiction.

To the unenlightened mind, it is.

What do you mean?

Well, to understand that this is not a contradiction, you have to experience the enlightened mind directly for yourself. The unenlightened mind simply cannot contain the paradox. That mind exists in and as duality itself, and therefore, by definition, cannot see beyond it to that place where no duality exists. You see, these two truths—that everything is already perfect and that everything must change—are simply different sides of the same coin. Ultimately, there is only one truth, but it appears differently depending on which side of the coin you are looking at. From an absolute point of view, everything is always already perfect, and that is enlightenment. From a relative point of view, everything must change because that is the law of the created universe, and that is enlightenment also. The mind that exists in and as duality can only see one of these truths at a time. But the mind that has been enlightened can perceive both simultaneously in the recognition that they are not separate.

Well, since my mind is not yet enlightened, which side of the coin is more important to give my attention to? That everything is perfect or that everything must change?

That's like asking which half of my heart is more important—
the question just doesn't make sense. They are different
manifestations of the *same* truth. Two sides of the same
one coin.

But my mind just can't get it.

They are equally important because they are equally true.
Genuine spiritual awakening is the profound and overwhelming discovery of the primordial ground of reality itself.
That ground is where there is no time, where the unmanifest,
unborn Self abides in the consciousness of absolute zero, or
no thing whatsoever. In the awakened state, that primordial
ground emerges in consciousness as the direct experience of
everything being perfect just as it is.

But genuine spiritual awakening is *also* the explosive
emergence of the evolutionary impulse in human consciousness. With the submission of the ego and the surrender of the
personal will, the individual becomes aware of the presence
of a powerful and unyielding energy. That energy is the
movement of the life-force in a self-propelled state of conscious evolution or becoming.

From absolutely Nothing, suddenly Something emerged,
and that Something has remained ever since in a constant
state of becoming. The source and ground of everything that
has become, and that is even now in a constant state of
becoming, is that place where there is no time and where
nothing ever happened. Nothing and Something cannot be
separated because they are simply two sides of the same one

coin. That's the meaning of nonduality and that is what enlightenment is: The awakened knowledge of this living mystery that cannot be divided.

the imperative to evolve 20

Q *Andrew, I have one last question, and as you would say, it's a big one... I really want to know where is all this leading? Ultimately, what is the purpose of enlightenment?*

A That's simple. Evolution!

But what exactly does that mean?

As I have been saying, in profound spiritual awakening a mysterious compulsion is activated in human consciousness. It is experienced as a call or command that arises spontaneously from the Self, as a powerful impulse to create order out of disorder, to manifest higher and higher expressions of harmony and integration as ourselves, in this world, for the sake of all of life.

What activates this "mysterious compulsion"?

Ego death!

What do you mean?

When the relentless will of the separate ego has finally been broken, the evolutionary impulse begins to become active within consciousness. That impulse is always there, but as long as we are hypnotized by the ego's agenda of unending self-concern, we remain oblivious to its presence. Indeed, as long as we remain lost in the nightmare of unconsciousness that is ego, it will be impossible to find out who we really are and why we are here.

So you're saying that when we awaken, we find out who we are and why we are here?

Yes. When we discover that primordial ground beyond the mind, we find out who we are. When the separate ego is transcended for real, we become aware of the evolutionary impulse and we know why we are here. And it is the direct experience of that primordial ground beyond the mind that sets us free—sets us free to finally be fully available to participate in the evolutionary process.

I do begin to sense that there is a great purpose in being here but I guess my question is, what would it look like?

Well, ideally it would look just like *you!*

Huh?

Why not? I mean, if you take what I've been saying seriously, it would *have* to look like you, wouldn't it?

Yes, I suppose it would.

Because?

Because I would realize that the evolution of the human race starts with me?

It doesn't start with you; it *is* you. It's just that you don't know it yet. Listen, you and I, right now, are participating in an extraordinary event that is in a miraculous process of endlessly *becoming*. And the most important part of that becoming is the evolution of consciousness itself. Don't you see what I'm getting at? That means *you*. How aware are you right now of the vast evolutionary process that you are participating in? You see, the human experience only begins to make deep and profound sense when we begin to *consciously* participate in the process that we are already a part of.

But how do I get in touch with this for myself?

You already are. The awakening of the longing for liberation in the human heart and mind is the first step toward becoming a conscious participant in the evolutionary process. Wholeheartedly responding to that longing is what makes it possible to literally become one with the process itself.

Becoming one with the evolutionary process—that's where all this is leading? That's what the purpose of enlightenment is?

The purpose of enlightenment is for us to become so conscious that, through our wholehearted participation, we actually begin to actively guide the evolutionary process itself. As outrageous as that sounds, it's true. You see, we are all desperately needed. Consciousness cannot evolve beyond a certain point without our wholehearted and fully conscious participation in the process. And for that to happen, we have to make ourselves available. That's why it's so, so important to want to be free more than anything else, not for ourselves but for the evolution of Life itself.

Learn more about the essential teachings
of Andrew Cohen in his acclaimed book
Embracing Heaven & Earth

"Andrew Cohen lays bare the process of spiritual growth, revealing
the workings of ego and the path to freedom with crystalline clarity.
He speaks with the resounding simplicity of all true masters. The
wisdom of the ages, freed here from cultural trappings, is delivered
with lightning bolts of uncompromising psychological insight. Any
seeker, whether grounded in a tradition or weary of religious conven-
tion, should read this remarkable, enlightening book."

Miranda Shaw, Ph.D.
author of *Passionate Enlightenment:
Women in Tantric Buddhism*

"The ring of truth in this book is like an alarm clock."

Lama Surya Das
author of *Awakening the Buddha Within*

Embracing Heaven & Earth · ISBN 1-883929-29-6 · $14.95
Call 800.376.3210 (US & Canada) or +1.413.637.6000 (outside US)
www.andrewcohen.org

The Impersonal Enlightenment Fellowship

Founded in 1988, the Impersonal Enlightenment Fellowship is a nonprofit organization inspired by the teachings of Andrew Cohen. This international community of students is united in a commitment to supporting Andrew's teaching work and to actualizing his revolutionary vision of Impersonal Evolutionary Enlightenment in every aspect of human life. The Impersonal Enlightenment Fellowship has centers in the United States, Europe, and Asia.

For more information about Andrew Cohen, his teachings, and IEF Centers around the world, please contact one of the Centers listed below or visit www.andrewcohen.org

Impersonal Enlightenment Fellowship

World Center
PO Box 2360
Lenox, MA 01240 USA
Tel: 1-413-637-6000
Fax: 1-413-637-6015
email: ief@andrewcohen.org

Impersonal Enlightenment Fellowship London

Centre Studios
Englands Lane
London NW3 4YD UK
Tel: 44-20-7419-8100
Fax: 44-20-7419-8101
email: ieflondon@andrewcohen.org

Note: IEF London will be moving in 2003.
For updated information please visit www.andrewcohen.org

about the author

Andrew Cohen has been a teacher of enlightenment since 1986. He is the author of numerous books on the spiritual life and founder of *What Is Enlightenment?* magazine, an award-winning forum for contemporary spiritual inquiry. Cohen continually travels the world giving talks and extended retreats and has met with visionary thinkers and spiritual leaders from every tradition. He is spiritual mentor to hundreds of students worldwide, and centers dedicated to his teachings can be found in Europe, Asia, and the United States, including an international retreat center in the Berkshire Hills of Western Massachusetts, where Cohen now has his home.

Andrew Cohen's other works include the acclaimed *Embracing Heaven & Earth, Freedom Has No History,* and *Enlightenment Is a Secret.*